The Glass

by Antonio Colantoni
illustrated by Mark Corcoran

Core Decodable 36

McGraw Hill Education

Bothell, WA • Chicago, IL • Columbus, OH • New York, NY

MHEonline.com

Send all inquiries to:
McGraw-Hill Education
8787 Orion Place
Columbus, OH 43240

ISBN: 978-0-02-140706-4
MHID: 0-02-140706-1

Printed in Canada.

9 10 11 12 KOD 24

Mom filled a glass.

As Mom rested, a bug smelled the glass.
What was in it?

The bug buzzed to its nest.

Bugs buzzed in a glass.

Bugs buzzed back to the nest.

Mom sat up and lifted the glass.
"I cannot sip!" said Mom.